Jump, Pup!

Susan B. Neuman

NATIONAL GEOGRAPHIC

Washington, D.C.

Vocabulary Tree

MY BACKYARD

ANIMALS

PETS

PUP

ACTIVITIES

play   jump   tug   run   roll   catch   wag
smell   see   walk   lie   nap

This is my pup. Let's play.

Jump, pup!

Tug!

Run.

Roll.

Catch a ball!

Catch a stick!

Wag your tail.

What do you smell?

Let's take a walk.

Let's see some friends.

Lie in the sun.

Yawn!

Take a nap.

YOUR TURN!

Tell a story about a pup.

Paperback ISBN: 978-1-4263-1508-4
Reinforced library edition ISBN: 978-1-4263-1509-1

Book design by David M. Seager

Photo credits

Cover, Tierfotoagentur/Alamy; 1, Close Encounters of the Furry Kind/Kimball Stock; 2–3, Gary Randall/Kimball Stock; 4, Jean-Michel Labat/ARDEA; 5, Jean-Michel Labat/ARDEA; 6, Renee Morris Animal Collection/Alamy; 7, Jean-Michel Labat/ARDEA; 8, Klein-Hubert/Kimball Stock; 9, Johan De Meester/ARDEA; 10–11, Stefanie Krause-Wieczorek/Imagebroker/Biosphoto; 12–13, Jean-Michel Sotto/Kimball Stock; 14–15, Jean-Michel Labat/ARDEA; 16, John Daniels/ARDEA; 17, Close Encounters of the Furry Kind/Kimball Stock; 18–19, Close Encounters of the Furry Kind/Kimball Stock; 20–21, Ron Kimball/Kimball Stock; 22, Gary Randall/Kimball Stock; 23 (top), John Daniels/ARDEA; 23 (puppy), John Daniels/ARDEA; 23 (ball), Stepan Bormotov/Shutterstock; 23 (bottom), Jean-Michel Labat/ARDEA; 24, Sabine Steuwer/Kimball Stock

National Geographic supports K–12 educators with ELA Common Core Resources.
Visit natgeoed.org/commoncore for more information.

Printed in the United States of America
22/WOR/11 (paperback)
22/WOR/4 (RLB)